German Christmas Cookbook

Crafting Christmas Memories with Timeless Recipes and Heartfelt Traditions from Germany

While every precaution has been taken in the preparation of this book, the publisher assumes no responsibility for errors or omissions, or for damages resulting from the use of the information contained herein.

FILIPINO DESSERT COOKBOOK

First edition. November 17, 2023.

ISBN: 979-8223934714

Written by john ahmad.

Table of Contents

John Ahmad

Chapter 1: Introduction to German Christmas Traditions

The Magic of German Christmas

The holiday season is a magical time of year, filled with warmth, joy, and cherished traditions. In Germany, Christmas is a time when communities come together to celebrate the season with an abundance of traditions that have been passed down through generations. In this chapter, we'll take a journey through the enchanting world of German Christmas traditions, learning about the customs, folklore, and the spirit that make this time of year so special in Germany.

Advent: A Season of Anticipation

German Christmas celebrations begin well before December 25th. Advent, which comes from the Latin word "adventus" meaning "arrival" or "coming," is the four-week period leading up to Christmas Day. It's a time of anticipation, reflection, and preparation for the birth of Christ. One of the most iconic symbols of Advent in Germany is the Advent wreath, which typically holds four candles, one of which is lit on each of the four Sundays leading up to Christmas. Each candle represents a different theme: hope, love, joy, and peace.

Advent Calendar: A popular tradition during this time is the Advent calendar. Children, and even adults, open a numbered door or window on the calendar each day in December leading up to Christmas. Behind each door, a small surprise or treat awaits, building excitement for the big day.

The Origins of German Christmas Traditions

Many of the Christmas traditions we associate with Germany today have deep historical roots. Some date back centuries, while others have evolved over time. Here are a few key elements that have shaped German Christmas traditions:

St. Nicholas Day (Nikolaustag): On the evening of December 5th, children in Germany place their shoes outside their doors, hoping that St. Nicholas will visit during the night and fill them with gifts, sweets, and small toys.

Christkind and Weihnachtsmann: In different regions of Germany, Christmas is brought by different gift-bringers. In the South, children receive gifts from the Christkind, often depicted as an angelic figure. In other parts, the Weihnachtsmann (Father Christmas) is the one who delivers presents.

Christmas Markets (Weihnachtsmärkte): These festive markets, held in towns and cities throughout Germany, are a highlight of the holiday season. Visitors can stroll through stalls filled with handmade crafts, decorations, and delicious seasonal treats like Glühwein (mulled wine) and roasted chestnuts.

Christmas Trees (Weihnachtsbaum): The tradition of decorating evergreen trees for Christmas has its origins in Germany. The first recorded Christmas tree was in Strasbourg, which is now part of France but was historically part of the Holy Roman Empire.

Regional Variations in Christmas Celebrations

One of the fascinating aspects of German Christmas traditions is their regional diversity. Germany is made up of different states, each with its own unique customs and culinary specialties. For example:

- In Bavaria, you might find a nativity scene with a crib and figurines carved from wood.
- In the Erzgebirge region, intricate wooden ornaments and pyramids are traditional decorations.
- The Rhineland is known for its lively and colorful parades called "Nikolausumzüge."
- In the Silesian region, you might encounter the tradition of "Rauhnächte," where people perform rituals to ward off evil spirits during the twelve nights between Christmas and Epiphany.

Throughout this cookbook, we'll explore these regional differences, bringing you a taste of the rich tapestry of German Christmas traditions.

As we delve deeper into the heart of German Christmas, you'll discover how these traditions influence the flavors and dishes that define this festive season. So, let's embark on this culinary and cultural journey through the pages of the "German Christmas Cookbook," where we'll not only learn to prepare delicious German holiday recipes but also gain a deeper appreciation for the traditions that make this time of year so special.

Chapter 2: Essential Ingredients and Kitchen Tools

Must-Have Ingredients for a German Christmas

When it comes to preparing the delightful dishes of a German Christmas, the right ingredients are the key to capturing the authentic flavors of this festive season. In this chapter, we'll explore the essential components that make up the backbone of German holiday cuisine, from traditional meats to seasonal produce.

Must-Have Ingredients for a German Christmas

1. Cinnamon: This warm and aromatic spice is a cornerstone of German Christmas baking. Ground cinnamon adds a comforting, sweet note to cookies, cakes.

2. Nutmeg: Freshly grated nutmeg elevates the flavor of many Christmas desserts and savory dishes. It's often used in stollen, potato dishes, and spiced wines.

3. Cloves: Ground or whole cloves infuse dishes with a rich, earthy flavor. They're a common addition to gingerbread cookies, holiday ham glazes, and mulled beverages.

4. Allspice: With its unique blend of flavors reminiscent of cloves, cinnamon, and nutmeg, allspice is a versatile spice in German Christmas cuisine. It's used in fruitcakes, sausages, and certain breads.

5. Anise: Anise seeds or star anise provide a licorice-like flavor, enhancing cookies, breads, and beverages. They're often used in springerle cookies and mulled cider.

6. Marzipan: This sweet almond paste is a beloved ingredient in German Christmas confections. It's shaped into fruits, figures, or used as a filling in stollen and other desserts.

7. Almonds: Ground almonds or almond flakes are prevalent in cookies, cakes, and sweet breads. They provide a delightful nuttiness and texture.

8. Raisins and Dried Fruits: Essential for stollen, fruitcakes, and other holiday treats. Soak them in rum or brandy for an extra layer of flavor.

9. Candied Citrus Peel: Used in stollen and fruitcakes, candied citrus peel adds a burst of citrusy sweetness and chewy texture.

10. Lebkuchengewürz: This is a blend of spices specifically for gingerbread and Lebkuchen cookies. It typically includes cinnamon, cloves, allspice, and ginger.

11. Baker's Ammonia (Hirschhornsalz): An old-fashioned leavening agent used in traditional German cookies like springerle. It imparts a unique texture and flavor.

12. Fresh Yeast: For bread baking, fresh yeast is preferred over dry yeast for its ability to create a soft, chewy crumb.

13. Potatoes: A staple in many German dishes, potatoes are used for dumplings, potato salads, and various sides.

14. Apples: A symbol of the harvest season, apples are used in desserts, compotes, and as a stuffing for meats like goose or duck.

15. Red Cabbage: Essential for creating the vibrant and tangy side dish known as Rotkohl or Blaukraut.

16. Sauerkraut: A beloved accompaniment to sausages and meats, sauerkraut provides a sour and crunchy contrast.

17. Mustard: German mustard varieties range from mild to spicy and are a favorite condiment for sausages and sandwiches.

18. Flour: High-quality all-purpose flour is used for baking cookies, cakes, and bread.

19. Sugar: Granulated, powdered, and brown sugars are used for sweetening various recipes.

20. Butter: Unsalted butter is a crucial ingredient for creating rich and buttery pastries.

Special Spices and Seasonings

Note: Many of these spices and seasonings have been mentioned in the list of must-have ingredients, but they are worth emphasizing due to their significance in German Christmas cooking.

Vanilla: Vanilla beans or extract are often used in cookies, cakes, and custards for a sweet and aromatic flavor.

Cardamom: Particularly important in Scandinavian and Northern German recipes, cardamom adds a unique, spicy-sweet note to baked goods.

Juniper Berries: Used in marinades for meats like venison and in sauerkraut dishes, juniper berries contribute a distinctive, piney flavor.

Bay Leaves: A common seasoning for soups and stews, bay leaves add depth to savory dishes.

Fresh Herbs: Herbs like parsley, thyme, and rosemary are used to season meats and side dishes.

Essential Kitchen Tools and Equipment

Having the right tools in your kitchen is essential for preparing German Christmas recipes efficiently and with precision. Here are some essential kitchen items:

1. Stand Mixer or Hand Mixer: Essential for whipping up cookie doughs, cake batters, and whipped cream.

2. Baking Sheets and Pans: A variety of sizes and types for cookies, bread, and roasts.

3. Mixing Bowls: Different sizes for ingredient prep, mixing, and storing.

4. Rolling Pins: For rolling out dough for cookies and pastry.

5. Cookie Cutters: Various shapes for creating festive cookies.

6. Pastry Brushes: Used for applying glazes, egg washes, and butter.

7. Piping Bags and Tips: For decorating cookies, cakes, and desserts.

8. Roasting Pan: Necessary for preparing meats like goose, duck, or pork roasts.

9. Graters and Zesters: For grating fresh nutmeg, citrus zest, and cheese.

10. Sifters: To ensure dry ingredients are clump-free and well-mixed.

11. Food Processor: Handy for chopping nuts, mixing dough, and making breadcrumbs.

12. Candy Thermometer: Essential for accurate temperature control when making candies and syrups.

13. Thermometer: Used to check the internal temperature of meats, especially for roasts and poultry.

14. Potato Ricer: Perfect for creating smooth mashed potatoes and potato dumplings.

15. Sausage Stuffer: If you plan to make your own sausages, this tool is a must.

16. Bread Baking Equipment: Including a bread pan, dough scraper, and a baking stone.

17. Cutting Boards and Knives: High-quality knives and cutting boards are crucial for efficient and safe food preparation.

18. Sieve or Strainer: Used for draining and straining ingredients like boiled potatoes and vegetables.

19. Measuring Cups and Spoons: Accurate measurements are vital for baking.

20. Spice Grinder: For freshly grinding whole spices like cloves and cardamom.

Where to Source Authentic Ingredients

Finding authentic German ingredients can be an exciting part of preparing traditional holiday dishes. Here are some tips on where to find them:

Specialty Grocery Stores: Look for international or German specialty stores in your area. They often carry a wide selection of authentic ingredients, from spices to marzipan.

Online Retailers: Many online stores offer German food products and ingredients, including specialty spices and seasonings.

Farmers' Markets: Fresh produce like apples, potatoes, and cabbage can often be found at local farmers' markets.

Butcher Shops: For high-quality sausages and meats, consider visiting a local butcher shop.

Bakeries: Some bakeries may offer freshly baked stollen and other German breads during the holiday season.

Imported Goods Stores: Stores specializing in imported foods may carry a variety of German ingredients.

With the right ingredients and kitchen tools at your disposal, you're well-prepared to embark on your culinary journey through the flavors of a German Christmas. In the upcoming chapters, we'll dive into recipes that utilize these ingredients and tools to create delicious holiday dishes that will transport you to the heart of Germany.

Chapter 3: Classic German Christmas Cookies

Buttery and Spiced: An Introduction to German Cookies

German Christmas cookies, known as "Weihnachtsplätzchen," are a beloved part of holiday traditions. These cookies are not only delicious but also a joy to make and share with loved ones. In this chapter, we'll delve into the world of German Christmas cookies, exploring their history, flavors, and the art of baking and decorating these delightful treats.

Buttery and Spiced: An Introduction to German Cookies

When you think of German Christmas cookies, think of a delightful combination of buttery richness and a warm, spiced aroma that fills the kitchen during the holiday season. These cookies are often small in size but bursting with flavor, making them the perfect sweet treats to enjoy with a cup of mulled wine, hot cocoa, or a steaming cup of coffee.

Key Ingredients:

Butter: German Christmas cookies are known for their rich, buttery flavor. High-quality unsalted butter is the foundation of these delectable treats.

Spices: Traditional spices like cinnamon, nutmeg, cloves, and allspice add warmth and depth to the cookies' flavor profile.

Nuts: Almonds and hazelnuts are common additions, contributing a delightful crunch and nutty undertone.

Citrus Zest: Lemon or orange zest infuses cookies with a bright and refreshing note.

Jam and Fruit Preserves: These are often used as fillings for sandwich cookies or as a glaze for Linzer cookies.

Recipes for Iconic German Christmas Cookies

Now, let's explore some of the most iconic German Christmas cookies that have been cherished for generations. These recipes will guide you through the process of creating these beloved treats in your own kitchen:

1. Vanillekipferl (Vanilla Crescent Cookies)

These crescent-shaped cookies are delicately flavored with vanilla and coated in powdered sugar. They melt in your mouth with each bite.

2. Lebkuchen (German Gingerbread Cookies)

These spiced cookies, reminiscent of gingerbread, are a holiday staple. They come in various shapes and sizes and can be glazed or decorated with icing.

3. Zimtsterne (Cinnamon Stars)

Cinnamon stars are gluten-free cookies made with ground almonds, egg whites, and a generous dusting of cinnamon. They are both chewy and crisp, with a wonderful nutty flavor.

4. Heidesand (German Brown Sugar Cookies)

Heidesand cookies are simple yet delightful. Made with brown sugar and butter, they have a sandy texture and a caramelized flavor.

5. Linzer Cookies

These sandwich cookies feature a buttery, nutty crust with a center filled with raspberry or apricot jam. The top cookie often has a decorative cutout.

6. Springerle

Springerle are embossed anise-flavored cookies, often with intricate designs. They're made using special molds or rolling pins and are perfect for gifting.

7. Spekulatius (German Spice Cookies)

Spekulatius are thin, crisp cookies flavored with a blend of spices, including cinnamon, cloves, and nutmeg. They are traditionally imprinted with intricate designs.

[8. Bethmännchen (Marzipan Cookies)

Bethmännchen are small marzipan cookies with almond halves for decoration. They have a delightful almond flavor and are often associated with Frankfurt.

9. Pfeffernüsse (Peppernuts)

Pfeffernüsse are small, spicy cookies that pack a punch with black pepper and spices. They're typically coated in powdered sugar.

Decorating Techniques and Tips

Decorating German Christmas cookies can be a creative and enjoyable activity. Here are some techniques and tips to make your cookies look as good as they taste:

Icing: Royal icing can be used to create intricate designs, flood cookies with color, and add delicate details.

Sprinkles and Nuts: Sprinkle colored sugar, chopped nuts, or edible glitter on cookies while the icing is still wet to add texture and visual appeal.

Dusting: Dust cookies with powdered sugar for a snowy effect, or use stencils to create patterns.

Drizzling: Melted chocolate or icing can be drizzled over cookies for a decorative touch.

Edible Decorations: Use edible gold or silver leaf, colored gels, or edible markers to add intricate details to your cookies.

Packaging and Gifting Homemade Cookies

Homemade cookies make thoughtful and heartfelt gifts during the holiday season. Here are some ideas for packaging and presenting your German Christmas cookies:

Cookie Tins: Store cookies in decorative tins that can be reused or kept as keepsakes.

Cellophane Bags: Place a selection of cookies in clear cellophane bags and tie them with festive ribbons.

Cookie Boxes: Choose festive holiday-themed boxes and arrange cookies neatly inside.

Cookie Jars: Fill decorative cookie jars with an assortment of your homemade treats.

Gift Baskets: Create customized gift baskets with an array of cookies, a jar of jam, or a bottle of mulled wine.

Homemade Labels: Attach labels with the names of each cookie variety and any special dietary information.

Now that you're equipped with the knowledge of these delightful German Christmas cookies, it's time to roll up your sleeves, preheat your oven, and start baking. Whether you're baking them for your own enjoyment, to share with family and friends, or to give as gifts, these cookies are sure to add a touch of German holiday magic to your celebrations.

Chapter 4: Stollen and Other Festive Breads

The History of Stollen

When it comes to German Christmas bread, few loaves are as iconic as Stollen. This rich, sweet bread has a history dating back centuries and is deeply intertwined with German Christmas traditions. In this chapter, we'll explore the fascinating history of Stollen, learn how to make a classic Stollen, discover variations of German Christmas bread, and dive into the art of perfecting bread baking.

The History of Stollen

Stollen, also known as Christstollen or Weihnachtsstollen, originated in the city of Dresden, Germany. Its history can be traced back to the 14th century, making it one of the oldest documented Christmas breads in Europe. The name "Stollen" is derived from the German word "Stolle," meaning a support or post, referring to the loaf's shape resembling a swaddled baby Jesus.

During its long history, Stollen has undergone various transformations. Initially, it was a plain, unleavened bread, as the Catholic Church had imposed strict fasting rules during Advent. However, in the 15th century, Pope Nicholas V granted the Duke of Saxony permission to use butter and milk in Stollen, and the bread evolved into the rich, fruit-filled loaf we know today.

Stollen Festival: Dresden's annual Stollen Festival, known as the "Stollenfest," celebrates this beloved bread. A giant Stollen, often weighing several tons, is paraded through the city and ceremoniously cut. Pieces of the giant Stollen are then distributed to the public.

Classic Stollen Recipe

Note: Making Stollen is a labor of love, and it's often prepared well in advance of Christmas. The flavors meld and develop over time.

Ingredients:

For the Stollen:

- 3 1/2 cups (440g) all-purpose flour
- 1/3 cup (70g) granulated sugar
- 2 1/4 tsp active dry yeast
- 3/4 cup (180ml) warm milk
- 1/2 cup (115g) unsalted butter, softened
- 1 large egg
- 1 tsp vanilla extract
- 1/2 tsp salt
- 1/2 tsp grated lemon zest
- 1/2 cup (75g) raisins
- 1/2 cup (75g) currants
- 1/2 cup (75g) candied orange peel, chopped
- 1/2 cup (75g) candied lemon peel, chopped
- 1/2 cup (60g) chopped almonds
- 1/2 cup (60g) chopped candied cherries
- 1/2 tsp ground cinnamon
- 1/4 tsp ground nutmeg
- Powdered sugar, for dusting

For the Filling:

- 1/4 cup (30g) almond paste
- 2 tbsp unsalted butter, softened
- 1 tbsp granulated sugar

Instructions:

1. In a small bowl, combine the warm milk and yeast. Let it sit for about 5 minutes until foamy.
2. In a large mixing bowl, combine the flour, granulated sugar, and

salt.

3. Make a well in the center of the flour mixture and add the yeast mixture, softened butter, egg, and vanilla extract. Mix to form a dough.

4. Knead the dough on a floured surface for about 5-7 minutes until smooth and elastic. Place it in a greased bowl, cover, and let it rise in a warm place for 1-2 hours or until doubled in size.

5. In a separate bowl, combine the raisins, currants, candied orange peel, candied lemon peel, chopped almonds, candied cherries, ground cinnamon, and ground nutmeg.

6. Punch down the risen dough and turn it out onto a floured surface. Roll it into a rectangle about 10x14 inches (25x35 cm).

7. In a small bowl, mix together the almond paste, softened butter, and granulated sugar. Spread this mixture evenly over the rolled-out dough.

8. Sprinkle the fruit and nut mixture over the almond paste layer.

9. Roll up the dough tightly from the long side, sealing the seam.

10. Place the Stollen on a baking sheet lined with parchment paper and let it rise for another 30-45 minutes.

11. Preheat your oven to 350°F (175°C).

12. Bake the Stollen for 30-35 minutes or until golden brown.

13. Remove the Stollen from the oven and let it cool on a wire rack.

14. Once cooled, dust the Stollen generously with powdered sugar.

1. Wrap the Stollen in plastic wrap and then foil. Store it in a cool, dark place for at least a week or up to a month before serving. The flavors will continue to develop over time.

Variations of German Christmas Breads

While Stollen is the most famous German Christmas bread, there are other regional variations and breads to explore during the holiday season:

Dresdner Stollen: The classic Stollen hailing from Dresden, filled with a mixture of candied fruit, almonds, and marzipan.

Christstollen: A variation of Stollen from the region of Thuringia, often featuring almonds, citrus peel, and a dusting of powdered sugar.

Früchtebrot: A dense, dark fruit bread filled with dried fruits, nuts, and sometimes spices.

Lebkuchenbrot: A gingerbread-style bread, often cut into squares and adorned with a glaze or icing.

Butterzopf: A braided bread made with butter, milk, and eggs, similar to challah, and often enjoyed during Advent.

Baumkuchen: Known as "tree cake," this layered cake is made by coating layers of dough with a sweet glaze, resembling tree rings when sliced.

Perfecting the Art of Bread Baking

Baking bread, whether it's Stollen or another festive variety, requires attention to detail and some essential skills. Here are some tips to help you perfect the art of bread baking:

Proper Kneading: Kneading the dough until it's smooth and elastic is crucial for good bread texture. It develops gluten and ensures even rising.

Rising Time: Allow the dough to rise until it has doubled in size. The time can vary depending on factors like temperature and yeast activity.

Preheating the Oven: Always preheat your oven to the specified temperature before placing the bread inside. A properly preheated oven ensures even baking.

Cooling: Allow bread to cool on a wire rack after baking. This prevents the bottom from becoming soggy due to trapped steam.

Storage: Store bread in a cool, dry place. Avoid sealing it in airtight containers right after baking, as it can retain moisture and become stale.

With the knowledge of Stollen and other German Christmas breads, along with the techniques of successful bread baking, you're ready to embark on a delicious journey through the world of holiday bread. Whether you're making Stollen to celebrate a centuries-old tradition or exploring regional variations, the aromas and flavors of these breads are sure to enhance your festive season.

Chapter 5: Hearty Soups and Appetizers

Warming Soups for the Holiday Season

The chilly winter months call for comforting, hearty dishes to warm the soul. German Christmas celebrations are no exception, and soups and appetizers play a crucial role in setting the stage for a festive feast. In this chapter, we'll explore a selection of warming soups that evoke the spirit of the season and appetizers that kickstart your Christmas feast. Additionally, we'll provide tips for hosting a memorable soup and appetizer party.

Warming Soups for the Holiday Season

German Christmas soups are designed to chase away the winter chill and prepare the palate for the rich flavors of the main course. Here are some classic options to consider:

1. Kartoffelsuppe (Potato Soup)

A creamy, hearty soup made with potatoes, leeks, and sometimes bacon. It's comfort in a bowl, perfect for a cold winter's day.

2. Erbsensuppe (Split Pea Soup)

A thick, flavorful soup made with split peas, smoked ham hocks, and vegetables. It's a hearty choice that's sure to warm you up.

3. Gulaschsuppe (Goulash Soup)

Inspired by Hungarian goulash, this soup features tender beef, paprika, and vegetables in a rich broth. It's both spicy and satisfying.

4. Kürbissuppe (Pumpkin Soup)

Creamy and velvety, pumpkin soup is often flavored with warming spices like nutmeg and cinnamon. It's a delightful way to celebrate the season's harvest.

5. Rote Linsensuppe (Red Lentil Soup)

A vegetarian option made with red lentils, tomatoes, and aromatic spices. It's both nutritious and delicious.

6. Weißwurstsuppe (White Sausage Soup)

A Bavarian specialty, this soup features delicate white sausages simmered in a flavorful broth with vegetables and herbs.

Appetizers to Kickstart Your Christmas Feast

Appetizers set the tone for your Christmas meal, offering a tantalizing preview of the flavors to come. Here are some appetizers that will delight your guests:

1. Sauerbraten Meatballs

Bite-sized meatballs made with the flavors of traditional sauerbraten, served with a tangy sauce for dipping.

2. Brezeln (Pretzels)

Soft pretzels served warm with mustard or a cheese dip. They're a crowd-pleaser and a great snack for mingling.

3. Herring Salad (Heringssalat)

A classic German appetizer featuring herring fillets, apples, onions, and a creamy dressing.

4. Obatzda

A Bavarian cheese spread made with Camembert or Brie, butter, onions, and spices. Serve with pretzels or bread.

5. Bratwurst Bites with Mustard

Mini bratwurst sausages cooked to perfection and served with a variety of mustards for dipping.

6. Kartoffelpuffer (Potato Pancakes)

Crispy potato pancakes served with applesauce or sour cream. They're a delightful and comforting appetizer.

Tips for Hosting a Soup and Appetizer Party

Hosting a soup and appetizer party can be a delightful way to celebrate the holiday season with friends and family. Here are some tips to ensure your gathering is a success:

Variety: Offer a variety of soups and appetizers to cater to different tastes and dietary preferences.

Presentation: Pay attention to presentation, using festive platters and garnishes to make your dishes visually appealing.

Timing: Serve the appetizers and soups in stages, allowing guests to savor each dish before moving on to the next.

Accompaniments: Provide an array of accompaniments like crusty bread, crackers, and condiments to complement the appetizers and soups.

Beverages: Offer a selection of beverages, including mulled wine, hot cider, and non-alcoholic options for guests of all ages.

Cozy Atmosphere: Set the mood with festive decorations, candles, and soft background music to create a cozy and welcoming ambiance.

With these soups, appetizers, and hosting tips, you're well-prepared to kickstart your Christmas feast and create memorable moments with your loved ones. In the following chapters, we'll explore traditional meat dishes, vegetarian delights, and a wide array of side dishes to complete your German Christmas menu.

Chapter 6: Traditional Meat Dishes for Christmas Eve

Roasts and Poultry: Main Courses for Christmas Eve

Christmas Eve is a time for indulgence and celebration, and German cuisine offers a delectable array of meat dishes to make this evening truly special. In this chapter, we'll explore the main courses that take center stage on Christmas Eve, discover traditional German stuffing and sauces, find sides that perfectly complement meat dishes, and learn how to create a festive Christmas Eve dinner menu.

Roasts and Poultry: Main Courses for Christmas Eve

German Christmas Eve dinners often feature hearty and flavorful meat dishes that are the highlight of the evening. Here are some classic options to consider:

1. Gänsebraten (Roast Goose)

Roast goose is a traditional centerpiece for Christmas Eve in many German households. It's often seasoned with a flavorful mixture of spices and herbs, resulting in crispy skin and succulent meat.

2. Entenbraten (Roast Duck)

Roast duck is another popular choice, often stuffed with a mixture of apples, onions, and herbs. The meat is tender, and the skin can become wonderfully crispy when prepared correctly.

3. Rinderbraten (Roast Beef)

A classic roast beef is marinated, seared, and slowly roasted to perfection. It's often served with a rich gravy made from pan drippings.

4. Schweinebraten (Roast Pork)

Roast pork is seasoned with a flavorful rub and slow-roasted until the meat is tender and the skin is crispy. It's a beloved dish in many regions of Germany.

5. Lammbraten (Roast Lamb)

Roast lamb, typically flavored with garlic and rosemary, is a favorite in some parts of Germany. It's an elegant choice for a Christmas Eve dinner.

6. Wildgerichte (Game Dishes)

In some regions, game dishes like venison or wild boar are enjoyed during the Christmas season. They offer a unique and robust flavor.

German Stuffing and Sauces

Traditional German stuffing and sauces enhance the flavors of meat dishes. Here are some classic options:

1. Semmelknödel (Bread Dumplings)

These dumplings are made from bread cubes, eggs, milk, and herbs. They soak up the delicious pan juices and make for a wonderful side dish.

2. Rotkohl (Red Cabbage)

Sweet and tangy red cabbage is a classic accompaniment to meat dishes. It's often flavored with apples, vinegar, and spices.

3. Kartoffelklöße (Potato Dumplings)

Potato dumplings are soft and fluffy, often served with gravy or sauce. They make a hearty addition to the plate.

4. Bratensauce (Roast Gravy)

Gravy made from pan drippings is a must-have for roast meats. It adds depth and richness to the dish.

5. Sauerkraut (Fermented Cabbage)

Sauerkraut provides a tangy contrast to the richness of roast meats. It's a staple in many German meals.

Sides that Complement Meat Dishes

Pairing the right sides with your main course is essential for a well-rounded Christmas Eve dinner. Here are some sides that complement meat dishes:

1. Kartoffelsalat (Potato Salad)

German potato salad, often dressed with a warm bacon vinaigrette, is a classic side dish that's both comforting and flavorful.

2. Grünkohl (Kale)

Sautéed kale is a popular side dish in northern Germany, often served with smoked sausages or pork.

3. Knödel (Dumplings)

Dumplings made from potatoes, bread, or semolina can be served alongside meat dishes to soak up the delicious sauces.

4. Gemüse (Vegetables)

Roasted or steamed vegetables such as carrots, Brussels sprouts, and green beans can provide a colorful and nutritious addition to the meal.

5. Kartoffelpüree (Mashed Potatoes)

Creamy mashed potatoes are a classic side that pairs well with roast meats and gravy.

Creating a Festive Christmas Eve Dinner Menu

Putting together a memorable Christmas Eve dinner menu is all about balance and variety. Here's a sample menu to inspire your festive feast:

Appetizer:

- Herring Salad or Pretzels with Mustard

Main Course:

- Gänsebraten (Roast Goose) with Semmelknödel (Bread Dumplings) and Rotkohl (Red Cabbage)
- Or choose another roast or poultry dish from the options provided

Sides:

- Kartoffelsalat (Potato Salad)
- Gemüse (Steamed Vegetables)

Dessert:

- Finish the evening with a slice of homemade Stollen, Lebkuchen, or a festive Yule log cake.

With this menu, you'll create a memorable and indulgent Christmas Eve dinner that captures the essence of German holiday traditions.

Chapter 7: Vegetarian and Vegan Delights

Vegetarian and Vegan Options for Christmas

German Christmas celebrations are inclusive, with delicious options available for those who prefer vegetarian or vegan dishes. In this chapter, we'll explore the delightful world of vegetarian and vegan delights for the holiday season. Discover plant-based main courses, sides, salads, and desserts that are sure to satisfy everyone at your Christmas table.

Vegetarian and Vegan Options for Christmas

German cuisine offers a variety of plant-based ingredients and flavors that can be transformed into festive dishes. Here are some options for those seeking vegetarian and vegan choices:

1. Gemüsestrudel (Vegetable Strudel)

A flaky pastry filled with a medley of roasted or sautéed vegetables, herbs, and spices.

2. Linsenbraten (Lentil Roast)

A hearty lentil loaf seasoned with herbs and spices, often accompanied by a flavorful gravy.

3. Kartoffelsalat (German Potato Salad)

A warm potato salad made with vinegar, mustard, and herbs, perfect as a side dish or a main course.

4. Kartoffelsuppe (Potato Soup)

A comforting soup made with potatoes, leeks, and vegetable broth, garnished with fresh herbs.

5. Rotkohl (Red Cabbage)

A sweet and tangy side dish made with red cabbage, apples, and spices.

6. Kartoffelklöße (Potato Dumplings)

Soft and fluffy potato dumplings that pair well with vegetarian and vegan gravies.

Plant-Based Main Courses

Plant-based main courses are the stars of a vegetarian or vegan Christmas feast. Here are some options that capture the essence of the season:

1. Nussbraten (Nut Roast)

A hearty roast made with a mixture of nuts, vegetables, breadcrumbs, and spices, often shaped into a loaf.

2. Gemüselasagne (Vegetable Lasagna)

Layers of pasta, tomato sauce, roasted vegetables, and dairy-free cheese create a satisfying and comforting dish.

3. Tofurkey (Tofu Turkey)

A tofu-based roast stuffed with a flavorful mixture of herbs, vegetables, and breadcrumbs.

4. Vegan Roulade

A rolled and stuffed pastry filled with a mixture of vegetables, tofu, or seitan, often served with vegan gravy.

5. Kartoffelsalat (German Potato Salad)

As a main course, serve a larger portion of warm potato salad with additional toppings like marinated tofu or tempeh.

Sides and Salads for a Meatless Christmas

Complement your plant-based main course with sides and salads that are both delicious and satisfying:

1. Rotkohl (Red Cabbage)

This sweet and tangy cabbage side dish pairs beautifully with vegetarian and vegan roasts.

2. Gemüse (Steamed Vegetables)

Steamed or roasted vegetables seasoned with herbs and spices make a nutritious and colorful addition to your Christmas table.

3. Kartoffelsalat (German Potato Salad)

A classic warm potato salad, perfect as a side dish or a main course for a vegetarian or vegan meal.

4. Kartoffelsalat (Vegan German Potato Salad)

A dairy-free and egg-free version of German potato salad, suitable for vegans.

5. Grünkohlsalat (Kale Salad)

A hearty kale salad with a lemon vinaigrette and toppings like roasted nuts and dried cranberries.

Desserts without Animal Products

No Christmas feast is complete without a sweet ending, and there are plenty of vegan dessert options to choose from:

1. Vegan Stollen

A plant-based version of the classic Stollen, often made with almond milk, coconut oil, and dried fruits.

2. Vegan Lebkuchen (Gingerbread)

Spiced gingerbread cookies and cakes made without eggs or dairy.

3. Vegan Apfelstrudel (Apple Strudel)

A flaky pastry filled with spiced apples and raisins, often made with vegan butter.

4. Vegan Marzipan

Homemade marzipan made with almond meal, powdered sugar, and almond extract, perfect for shaping into festive figures or candies.

5. Vegan Zimtsterne (Cinnamon Stars)

These gluten-free cinnamon star cookies can be made with aquafaba (chickpea brine) instead of egg whites.

Creating a Festive Vegetarian or Vegan Christmas Menu

For a memorable vegetarian or vegan Christmas menu, consider the following options:

Appetizer:

A selection of vegan dips and spreads with fresh bread or crackers.

Main Course:

- Nussbraten (Nut Roast) with vegan gravy
- Gemüselasagne (Vegetable Lasagna)
- A vegan Tofurkey or roulade

Sides:

- Rotkohl (Red Cabbage)
- Steamed or roasted Gemüse (Vegetables)
- Vegan Kartoffelsalat (Potato Salad) or Kartoffelsalat (German Potato Salad)

Dessert:

- Vegan Stollen or Vegan Lebkuchen
- Vegan Apfelstrudel or Vegan Zimtsterne

With this menu, you'll create a festive and inclusive Christmas celebration where everyone can savor the flavors of the season.

Chapter 8: Side Dishes for a German Christmas Feast

A Variety of Sides to Complete Your Holiday Spread

A well-rounded Christmas feast is not complete without an array of delicious side dishes. In this chapter, we'll explore a variety of sides that complement both meat and plant-based main courses, enhancing your German Christmas table. From classic potato dishes to traditional German sauerkraut and red cabbage, and colorful vegetable side dishes, there's something for everyone to enjoy.

Potato Dishes: A German Staple

Potatoes are a beloved staple in German cuisine, and they make appearances in various forms on the Christmas table. Here are some classic potato dishes to consider:

1. Kartoffelsalat (German Potato Salad)

A warm potato salad made with vinegar, mustard, and herbs, often served as a side dish or a main course.

2. Kartoffelpüree (Mashed Potatoes)

Creamy mashed potatoes, a comforting and versatile side that pairs well with gravies and sauces.

3. Bratkartoffeln (Pan-Fried Potatoes)

Slices of potatoes pan-fried until crispy and golden, often seasoned with onions, bacon, and herbs.

4. Kartoffelgratin (Potato Gratin)

Sliced potatoes layered with cream and cheese, baked to perfection for a rich and decadent side dish.

5. Kartoffelsuppe (Potato Soup)

A comforting soup made with potatoes, leeks, and vegetable broth, garnished with fresh herbs.

Traditional German Sauerkraut and Red Cabbage

Sauerkraut and red cabbage are classic accompaniments to German Christmas meals, providing a sweet and tangy contrast to rich and savory main courses. Here's a closer look at these traditional side dishes:

1. Sauerkraut

Fermented cabbage that's tangy and often flavored with apples, onions, and sometimes a touch of sugar. It's a staple in German cuisine and pairs beautifully with roasts and sausages.

2. Rotkohl (Red Cabbage)

Sweet and tangy red cabbage, often simmered with apples, vinegar, and spices, adding a vibrant and flavorful element to the Christmas table.

Vegetable Side Dishes for Color and Flavor

Vegetable side dishes bring color, freshness, and variety to your Christmas feast. Here are some vegetable options to consider:

1. Grünkohl (Kale)

Sautéed or braised kale, often served with smoked sausages or pork for a hearty and nutritious side.

2. Gemüse (Steamed Vegetables)

Steamed or roasted vegetables like carrots, Brussels sprouts, green beans, or broccoli, seasoned with herbs and spices.

3. Spargel (Asparagus)

Asparagus, often served during the spring months in Germany, can also make a delightful addition to a festive Christmas spread.

4. Pilze (Mushrooms)

Sautéed mushrooms with herbs and garlic add earthy flavors and a delightful umami element to your meal.

5. Rote Bete (Beets)

Roasted or pickled beets can provide a colorful and slightly sweet component to your Christmas table.

Creating a Balanced Christmas Feast

To create a balanced Christmas feast, consider combining a variety of sides that complement your chosen main courses, whether they are meat-based or plant-based. A well-rounded selection of sides ensures that every guest at your table finds something to enjoy.

With these side dishes, you'll enhance the flavors and textures of your German Christmas feast, creating a memorable and satisfying holiday meal.

Chapter 9: The Art of German Sausages

Exploring the World of German Sausages

Sausages are an integral part of German cuisine, and they hold a special place on the Christmas table. In this chapter, we'll dive into the world of German sausages, from the various types and flavors to the art of cooking and serving them. You'll also find delicious sausage recipes perfect for the holidays and discover the ideal pairings with mustards and sauces.

Exploring the World of German Sausages

Germany is famous for its diverse and flavorful sausages, each region boasting its own unique variations. Here are some popular types of German sausages to explore:

1. Bratwurst

A staple across Germany, bratwurst is a type of fresh sausage made with pork, veal, or beef. It's seasoned with a blend of herbs and spices and typically grilled or pan-fried.

2. Weisswurst

A Bavarian specialty, weisswurst is a pale, mild sausage made with veal and pork. It's traditionally served with sweet mustard and pretzels.

3. Knackwurst

Known for its distinctive snap when bitten, knackwurst is a short, plump sausage made with a blend of meats and seasoned with garlic and spices.

4. Thüringer Rostbratwurst

Hailing from Thuringia, these sausages are known for their unique spice blend, including marjoram. They're often grilled and served in a roll.

5. Nürnberger Rostbratwurst

These small, thin sausages originate from Nuremberg. They're made with pork and spices, and a serving typically consists of multiple sausages.

Cooking and Serving German Sausages

Cooking and serving sausages is an art in itself. Here are some tips for preparing and presenting German sausages:

1. Grilling: Grilling is a popular method for cooking sausages. Preheat the grill to medium-high heat and cook the sausages until they're browned and cooked through, turning them occasionally.

2. Pan-Frying: Pan-frying is another common method. Heat a skillet over medium heat, add a bit of oil, and cook the sausages until they're golden brown and cooked through.

3. Boiling: Some sausages, like weisswurst, are traditionally boiled. Simmer them gently in hot water for about 10-15 minutes.

4. Serving: German sausages are often served with a variety of accompaniments, including mustard, sauerkraut, pickles, and fresh bread or pretzels.

Sausage Recipes for the Holidays

German sausages add a savory element to holiday feasts. Here are some recipes featuring sausages that are perfect for the holiday season:

1. Wurstsalat (Sausage Salad)

A refreshing salad made with thinly sliced sausages, onions, pickles, and a tangy vinaigrette dressing.

2. Kartoffelsuppe mit Wurst (Potato Soup with Sausage)

A hearty potato soup with chunks of sausage, perfect for warming up on a chilly winter evening.

3. Sausage and Sauerkraut Bake

A comforting casserole made with sausages, sauerkraut, and potatoes, baked to perfection.

4. Bratwurst with Sauerkraut and Mustard

Classic bratwurst served with a generous portion of sauerkraut and your choice of mustard.

5. Sausage and Cheese Platter

Create a festive sausage and cheese platter with a variety of sausages, cheeses, and condiments, ideal for holiday gatherings.

Sausage Pairings with Mustards and Sauces

Sausages come to life when paired with the right mustards and sauces. Here are some classic pairings to elevate your sausage experience:

1. Sweet Mustard

A mild and slightly sweet mustard, perfect for weisswurst and pretzels.

2. Spicy Mustard

A zesty, spicy mustard that adds a kick to bratwurst and knackwurst.

3. Grainy Mustard

A coarse, textured mustard that pairs well with most sausages, adding a delightful texture and flavor.

4. Sauerkraut

Tangy and fermented sauerkraut is a classic accompaniment to sausages, balancing their richness.

5. Horseradish Sauce

A creamy horseradish sauce adds a bold and pungent kick to sausages, particularly bratwurst.

Whether you're enjoying sausages as a snack, appetizer, or main course, the right pairings with mustards and sauces can elevate the experience.

Chapter 10: Indulgent Desserts and Cakes

Rich and Decadent German Desserts

A German Christmas feast wouldn't be complete without a selection of indulgent desserts and cakes to satisfy your sweet tooth. In this chapter, we'll explore the world of rich and decadent German desserts, provide you with cake recipes suitable for special occasions, share tips for dessert presentation and garnishes, and even suggest dessert wine pairings to enhance your culinary experience.

Rich and Decadent German Desserts

German desserts are celebrated for their rich flavors and textures. Here are some classic indulgent options to consider for your holiday table:

1. Schwarzwälder Kirschtorte (Black Forest Cake)

Layers of chocolate sponge cake soaked in cherry brandy, filled with whipped cream and cherries, and garnished with chocolate shavings.

2. Apfelstrudel (Apple Strudel)

Thin layers of flaky pastry wrapped around a spiced apple filling, often served warm with a dusting of powdered sugar and a scoop of vanilla ice cream.

3. Rote Grütze

A vibrant red berry compote made with a variety of summer berries, often served with vanilla sauce or whipped cream.

4. Kaiserschmarrn

A fluffy, torn pancake served with powdered sugar and fruit preserves, perfect for sharing.

5. Dampfnudeln

Sweet, steamed dumplings served with a warm vanilla custard sauce.

6. Marzipan

Almond paste marzipan is used to create a variety of confections, from candies to marzipan fruits and holiday treats.

Cake Recipes for Special Occasions

Special occasions call for special cakes. Here are some cake recipes that will shine on your holiday table:

1. Stollen

A festive fruit and nut-filled bread that's coated in powdered sugar, making it a Christmas classic.

2. Lebkuchen (Gingerbread)

Soft and spiced gingerbread cakes, often decorated with icing or glaze.

3. Dresdner Christstollen (Dresden Stollen)

A variation of Stollen hailing from Dresden, known for its dense, rich texture and abundant fruit and nut fillings.

4. Nusstorte (Nut Torte)

A layered nut torte filled with a creamy, nutty filling, often topped with chocolate

or icing.

5. Bienenstich (Bee Sting Cake)

A honey and almond cake filled with a creamy custard or buttercream, featuring a caramelized almond topping.

6. Pfeffernüsse

Spiced, chewy cookies often enjoyed during the holiday season.

German Dessert Presentation and Garnishes

The presentation of desserts adds to their allure. Here are some tips for presenting and garnishing your German desserts:

1. Powdered Sugar

A light dusting of powdered sugar adds elegance to many desserts, including strudels and pancakes.

2. Whipped Cream

A dollop of fresh whipped cream is a classic accompaniment to many German desserts.

3. Chocolate Shavings

Use a grater to create delicate chocolate shavings to adorn cakes like Black Forest Cake.

4. Fresh Berries

A few fresh berries can add a burst of color and freshness to your dessert plate.

5. Mint Leaves

A sprig of fresh mint adds a touch of green and a refreshing aroma to your presentation.

Chapter 11: Homemade Hot Drinks

Hot Chocolate and Other Hot Drinks

As the holiday season approaches, there's nothing quite like sipping on a warm, comforting drink to ward off the winter chill. In this chapter, we'll explore homemade hot drink recipes, from classic hot chocolate to other delightful hot beverages that will keep you cozy during the holidays. We'll also provide non-alcoholic options suitable for all ages.

Hot Chocolate and Other Hot Drinks

Hot chocolate is a beloved winter treat that's perfect for sipping by the fire or while watching snowfall. Here's a classic recipe for homemade hot chocolate:

Classic Homemade Hot Chocolate

Ingredients:

- 2 cups whole milk
- 1/2 cup heavy cream
- 4 ounces semi-sweet chocolate, finely chopped
- 2 tablespoons unsweetened cocoa powder
- 2 tablespoons granulated sugar (adjust to taste)
- 1 teaspoon pure vanilla extract
- A pinch of salt
- Whipped cream and chocolate shavings for garnish (optional)

Instructions:

1. In a saucepan over medium-low heat, combine the milk and heavy cream. Heat until it's steaming but not boiling.
2. In a separate bowl, whisk together the finely chopped chocolate, cocoa powder, sugar, and salt.

1. Slowly add the dry mixture to the steaming milk, whisking constantly until the chocolate and cocoa are completely melted

and the mixture is smooth and creamy.

2. Remove from heat and stir in the vanilla extract.

3. Pour the hot chocolate into mugs and top with whipped cream and chocolate shavings, if desired. Serve immediately.

Other Hot Drink Options

While hot chocolate is a classic, consider adding variety to your hot drink offerings with these options:

Kinderpunsch: A non-alcoholic punch for kids and non-drinkers, made with fruit juices like apple and grape, and flavored with spices.

Heiße Schokolade mit Schuss (Hot Chocolate with a Shot): Add a touch of your favorite liqueur, such as peppermint schnapps, amaretto, or Irish cream, to your hot chocolate for an adult twist.

Chai Tea: Brew a comforting cup of chai tea with spices like cinnamon, cardamom, and cloves, sweetened with honey or sugar and enriched with milk.

Punsch (Punch): A warm and fruity punch made with fruit juices, spices, and sometimes a splash of rum or schnapps for adults.

Non-Alcoholic Options for All Ages

It's essential to have non-alcoholic hot drink options for all ages, especially when hosting family gatherings. Here are some delightful non-alcoholic options:

1. Kinderpunsch (Kid's Punch)

Ingredients:

- 2 cups apple juice
- 1 cup grape juice
- 1/2 cup orange juice
- 1 cinnamon stick
- 4 cloves
- 2-3 slices of lemon
- 2-3 slices of orange
- 2 tablespoons honey (optional, adjust to taste)

Instructions:

1. In a saucepan, combine the apple juice, grape juice, and orange juice.
2. Add the cinnamon stick, cloves, lemon slices, and orange slices.
3. Heat the mixture over low heat until it's warm, but do not boil.
4. If desired, add honey to sweeten the punch, stirring until it dissolves.
5. Serve the punch in mugs, garnished with a cinnamon stick or citrus slices.

2. Homemade Hot Apple Cider

Ingredients:

- 4 cups apple cider or apple juice
- 4 cinnamon sticks
- 4 whole cloves
- 2-3 slices of orange

Instructions:

1. In a saucepan, combine the apple cider or apple juice, cinnamon sticks, cloves, and orange slices.
2. Heat the mixture over low heat, allowing the flavors to infuse for about 15-20 minutes. Do not boil.
3. Serve the hot apple cider in mugs, garnished with a cinnamon stick or orange slice.

These non-alcoholic hot drink options are sure to be a hit with guests of all ages, making your holiday gatherings warm and enjoyable.

Chapter 12: Advent Calendar: A Sweet Countdown

The Advent Calendar Tradition

The Advent calendar is a cherished holiday tradition that builds excitement and anticipation for Christmas Day. In this chapter, we'll explore the history and significance of the Advent calendar, guide you in creating your own homemade Advent calendar, suggest delightful fillings of sweet surprises, and provide special activities for each day of this festive countdown.

The Advent Calendar Tradition

The Advent calendar traces its origins to 19th-century Germany. It was originally a way for families to mark the days leading up to Christmas by lighting candles, hanging religious images, or opening small doors in a calendar-style format. Today, Advent calendars come in various forms, including those with chocolates, toys, and even homemade surprises.

The Advent season typically begins on December 1st and lasts until December 24th, with each day bringing a new surprise or activity to celebrate the approaching Christmas Day.

Creating a Homemade Advent Calendar

Creating a homemade Advent calendar adds a personal touch to your holiday celebrations. Here's how to make one:

Materials Needed:

- 24 small envelopes or boxes
- Number stickers or markers
- A large poster or board
- Festive decorations (optional)
- String or ribbon
- Small clothespins or clips

Instructions:

1. Label each envelope or box with numbers 1 through 24. You can use number stickers, markers, or get creative with festive designs.
2. Decorate your large poster or board to serve as the backdrop for your Advent calendar. You can use wrapping paper, craft paper, or fabric to create an inviting display.
3. Arrange the envelopes or boxes on the poster or board in numerical order. You can create a tree shape, a garland, or any pattern you like.
4. Fill each envelope or box with a sweet surprise, a small toy, or a handwritten note describing an activity for the day.
5. Attach the envelopes or boxes to the poster or board using string or ribbon and small clothespins or clips.

Filling Your Calendar with Sweet Surprises

When it comes to filling your Advent calendar with sweet surprises, consider traditional German treats and holiday favorites:

1. Chocolate Truffles

Individually wrapped chocolate truffles, some with festive shapes and flavors like hazelnut or marzipan.

2. Lebkuchen (Gingerbread) Cookies

Miniature gingerbread cookies decorated with icing or sugar.

3. Marzipan

Small marzipan figures or candies, shaped like fruits, animals, or holiday symbols.

4. Chocolate Coins

Foil-wrapped chocolate coins, often used to mimic the appearance of real currency.

5. Stollen Bites

Bite-sized pieces of Stollen, the classic German Christmas bread, dusted with powdered sugar.

6. Candies and Confections

Assorted candies, pralines, or nougats in festive wrappers.

7. Miniature Advent Calendars

Mini Advent calendars within your larger calendar, with tiny surprises behind each door.

Special Activities for Each Day

In addition to sweet treats, consider including special activities for each day in your Advent calendar to make the countdown memorable:

1. Decorate Gingerbread Cookies

Have a family cookie decorating session with gingerbread cookies and colorful icing.

2. Write Letters to Santa

Dedicate a day to writing letters to Santa Claus, sharing your holiday wishes and gratitude.

3. Make a Holiday Craft

Create a simple holiday craft project together, such as paper ornaments or paper snowflakes.

4. Watch a Christmas Movie

Choose a beloved Christmas movie to watch as a family with hot chocolate and popcorn.

5. Visit a Christmas Market

If possible, plan a visit to a local Christmas market to experience the festive atmosphere.

6. Read a Christmas Story

Select a favorite Christmas story or book to read aloud before bedtime.

The combination of sweet surprises and special activities will make your homemade Advent calendar a cherished part of your holiday traditions.

With your Advent calendar ready to go, the countdown to Christmas becomes an exciting and joyful journey, bringing family and friends closer together in celebration of the season.

Chapter 13: DIY Christmas Decorations and Crafts

Crafting Your Own German Christmas Decorations

Creating your own Christmas decorations and crafts adds a personal and festive touch to your holiday celebrations. In this chapter, we'll explore the art of crafting German-inspired Christmas decorations, making handmade ornaments and decor, creating DIY Advent wreaths, and enjoying Christmas crafting with kids.

Crafting Your Own German Christmas Decorations

German Christmas decorations are renowned for their craftsmanship and charm. Here are some ideas for crafting your own:

1. Paper Stars (Froebelsterne)

Create intricate paper stars using colorful paper strips. Hang them from the ceiling or use them as window decorations to capture the essence of a German Christmas market.

2. Window Silhouettes (Fensterbilder)

Cut out simple silhouettes of Christmas scenes or figures from black paper. Attach them to your windows for a delightful play of light and shadow.

3. Candle Centerpieces

Design your own candle centerpieces by arranging candles of varying heights in a decorative manner. Consider adding natural elements like pinecones, holly, or evergreen branches.

4. Wooden Ornaments

Craft wooden ornaments in traditional shapes like stars, angels, or hearts. Paint or decorate them with intricate patterns to reflect German folk art.

5. Gingerbread House

Build and decorate your gingerbread house. Use royal icing and candies to create a delightful edible decoration for your table.

Handmade Ornaments and Decor

Handmade ornaments and decor add a personal and heartfelt touch to your Christmas tree and home. Here are some ideas:

1. Salt Dough Ornaments

Make salt dough ornaments by combining flour, salt, and water. Roll out the dough, cut it into shapes, bake until hardened, and then decorate with paint or markers.

2. Cinnamon Ornaments

Create fragrant cinnamon ornaments using a mixture of cinnamon, applesauce, and glue. Roll out the dough, cut shapes, and let them air dry for a rustic, scented decoration.

3. Felt Ornaments

Sew or glue together felt shapes to make charming ornaments. Consider crafting mini stockings, snowflakes, or animals to hang on the tree.

4. Pinecone Decorations

Collect pinecones and transform them into rustic decorations by painting them, adding glitter, or tying them with ribbon.

DIY Advent Wreaths

Crafting your own Advent wreath is a meaningful tradition. Here's how to make one:

Materials Needed:

- A circular wreath base (usually made of foam or grapevine)
- Four candles (three purple and one pink)
- Greenery (fresh or artificial)
- Pinecones, berries, or other natural elements
- Ribbon or fabric for embellishment

Instructions:

1. Attach the greenery to the wreath base, securing it with floral wire or hot glue.
2. Place the four candles evenly around the wreath, with the pink candle positioned among the three purple ones.
3. Decorate the wreath with pinecones, berries, or other natural elements to create a festive look.
4. Add ribbon or fabric as a final touch, tying bows or creating loops for hanging.

Christmas Crafting with Kids

Incorporating Christmas crafting with kids is a wonderful way to bond and create lasting memories. Here are some kid-friendly craft ideas:

1. Handprint Reindeer

Create reindeer decorations by having kids make handprints with brown paint or ink. Add eyes, antlers, and a red nose to complete the look.

2. Paper Plate Snow Globes

Turn paper plates into snow globes by painting or coloring winter scenes on them. Glue on cotton balls for a snowy effect.

3. Pasta Ornaments

Make ornaments using different shapes of pasta, painting them in festive colors and stringing them together with yarn.

4. Pinecone Christmas Trees

Collect pinecones and let kids paint them green. Add mini pom-poms as ornaments and a star at the top to create adorable mini Christmas trees.

5. Holiday Cards

Encourage kids to craft their own holiday cards using colored paper, markers, stickers, and glitter.

Crafting with kids fosters creativity and adds a joyful element to your holiday preparations.

With these DIY decoration and craft ideas, you can infuse your home with the warmth and beauty of a German-inspired Christmas, all while creating cherished memories with your loved ones.

Chapter 14: Celebrating with German Christmas Markets

The Enchantment of German Christmas Markets

German Christmas markets, or "Weihnachtsmärkte," are a quintessential part of the holiday season, offering a magical atmosphere, delightful treats, and unique gifts. In this chapter, we'll explore the enchantment of German Christmas markets, guide you in bringing the market experience home with DIY market stalls, provide recipes for traditional market foods you can make at home, and offer tips for planning a trip to Germany's Christmas markets.

The Enchantment of German Christmas Markets

German Christmas markets are a centuries-old tradition that brings communities together to celebrate the holiday season. Here's what makes them enchanting:

1. Festive Atmosphere

Christmas markets are adorned with twinkling lights, festive decorations, and the sweet scent of mulled wine and roasting chestnuts.

2. Unique Gifts

Artisans and vendors offer a wide array of handcrafted gifts, ornaments, and seasonal decor, making it an ideal place for holiday shopping.

3. Delightful Treats

The markets feature an abundance of traditional treats, from sausages and roasted nuts to gingerbread cookies and warm beverages.

4. Entertainment

Carolers, live music, and cultural performances add to the festive ambiance, making each market unique.

5. Community Spirit

Christmas markets foster a sense of community and togetherness, where families and friends gather to celebrate.

Bringing the Market Home: DIY Market Stalls

You can recreate the charm of a German Christmas market in your own home by crafting DIY market stalls:

Materials Needed:

- Cardboard boxes or wooden crates
- Craft paper or fabric for decoration
- Paints, markers, or stickers for signage
- String lights or LED candles
- Festive tablecloths

Instructions:

1. Choose a location in your home or yard to set up your DIY market stalls.
2. Transform cardboard boxes or wooden crates into stalls by cutting openings for windows and doors.
3. Decorate the stalls with craft paper or fabric to create a festive market facade.
4. Use paints, markers, or stickers to add signage with the names of the "vendors" or types of goods sold.
5. Add string lights or LED candles to create a warm and inviting atmosphere.
6. Drape festive tablecloths over tables or surfaces to display your market treats and crafts.

Traditional Market Foods to Make at Home

Recreate the flavors of a German Christmas market by making traditional market foods at home:

1. Bratwurst with Sauerkraut

Grill or pan-fry bratwurst sausages and serve them with sauerkraut and mustard.

2. Currywurst

Sliced bratwurst topped with a flavorful curry ketchup sauce and served with French fries.

3. Roasted Chestnuts

Roast chestnuts in the oven until the shells split open, and enjoy them warm with a sprinkle of salt.

4. Gingerbread Cookies

Bake gingerbread cookies in various shapes and decorate them with icing or sugar.

5. Gebrannte Mandeln (Candied Almonds)

Make candied almonds by caramelizing sugar and coating roasted almonds with the sweet syrup.

Planning a Trip to Germany's Christmas Markets

If you dream of experiencing Germany's Christmas markets firsthand, here are some tips for planning your trip:

1. Choose Your Destinations

Research the cities and regions in Germany that host renowned Christmas markets, such as Nuremberg, Munich, and Dresden.

2. Book Accommodations Early

Accommodations fill up quickly during the holiday season, so make reservations well in advance.

3. Check Dates and Hours

Christmas market schedules can vary by location, so check the dates and opening hours to plan your visit accordingly.

4. Pack Warm Clothing

German winters can be chilly, so pack warm clothing, including coats, scarves, and gloves.

5. Try Local Specialties

Sample regional specialties like Lebkuchen, Nürnberger sausages, and Glühwein while exploring the markets.

6. Explore the Surroundings

Many Christmas markets are located in historic city centers, so take time to explore the surrounding attractions.

Visiting Germany's Christmas markets is a magical experience that allows you to immerse yourself in the holiday spirit and create lasting memories.

Chapter 15: Gifts from the Kitchen: Homemade Food Gifts

Thoughtful Homemade Gifts for the Holidays

Homemade food gifts are a delightful way to share the warmth and flavors of the holiday season with friends and family. In this chapter, we'll explore the art of crafting thoughtful homemade gifts, provide packaging and presentation ideas to make your gifts extra special, share DIY food gift recipes, and guide you in creating personalized gift baskets.

Thoughtful Homemade Gifts for the Holidays

Homemade food gifts convey love and thoughtfulness, making them perfect for the holiday season. Here are some ideas for thoughtful gifts from your kitchen:

1. Spice Blends

Create custom spice blends for grilling, roasting, or seasoning, and package them in decorative jars.

2. Infused Oils and Vinegars

Infuse olive oils or vinegars with herbs, spices, or citrus zest for a gourmet touch.

3. Homemade Jams and Preserves

Cook up batches of fruit jams, jellies, or marmalades using seasonal fruits.

4. Flavored Salts

Craft unique flavored salts, such as rosemary-infused salt or smoky sea salt, for cooking enthusiasts.

5. Baking Mixes

Layer dry ingredients for cookies, brownies, or cakes in mason jars, complete with baking instructions.

6. Holiday Cookies

Bake an assortment of festive cookies and arrange them in decorative tins or boxes.

Packaging and Presentation Ideas

The presentation of your homemade food gifts is just as important as the contents. Here are some packaging and presentation ideas:

1. Mason Jars

Use mason jars for jams, baking mixes, or infused oils, and add a ribbon or fabric square for a rustic touch.

2. Decorative Tins

Choose festive tins or boxes to hold cookies, candies, or spice blends.

3. Cellophane Bags

Place cookies, candies, or granola in clear cellophane bags and tie with colorful ribbon.

4. Gift Baskets

Create gift baskets with an assortment of homemade treats and decorative filler.

5. Custom Labels

Design personalized labels with holiday-themed graphics and your recipient's name.

6. Handwritten Notes

Include a heartfelt handwritten note or recipe card to accompany your gift.

DIY Food Gift Recipes

Here are some DIY food gift recipes to inspire your holiday giving:

1. Homemade Vanilla Extract

Ingredients:

- 2-3 vanilla beans
- 8 ounces vodka or rum

Instructions:

1. Split the vanilla beans lengthwise and place them in a clean glass bottle or jar.
2. Pour the vodka or rum over the beans, ensuring they are fully submerged.
3. Seal the bottle or jar and store it in a cool, dark place for at least 6 weeks, shaking it occasionally.
4. Once ready, strain the extract and transfer it to smaller decorative bottles for gifting.

2. Rosemary and Lemon Infused Olive Oil

Ingredients:

- 2 sprigs of fresh rosemary
- Zest of 1 lemon
- 1 cup extra-virgin olive oil

Instructions:

1. Combine the rosemary sprigs and lemon zest in a clean glass bottle or jar.
2. Pour the olive oil over the rosemary and lemon.
3. Seal the bottle or jar and let it sit in a cool, dark place for at least 2 weeks.
4. Strain the infused oil and transfer it to decorative bottles for gifting.

3. Cranberry Orange Jam
Ingredients:

- 12 ounces fresh cranberries
- Zest and juice of 2 oranges
- 2 cups granulated sugar
- 1/2 teaspoon ground cinnamon

Instructions:

1. In a saucepan, combine the cranberries, orange zest, orange juice, sugar, and cinnamon.
2. Bring the mixture to a boil, then reduce the heat and simmer for about 15-20 minutes, or until the jam thickens.
3. Let the jam cool before transferring it to jars for gifting.

Creating Personalized Gift Baskets

For a truly personalized touch, create gift baskets with a selection of homemade treats and complementary items. Here's how:

1. Choose a Theme

Decide on a theme for your gift basket, such as "Holiday Brunch" or "Gourmet Cooking."

2. Select Homemade and Store-Bought Items

Include your homemade food gifts along with complementary store-bought items like cheeses, crackers, or wine.

3. Arrange Thoughtfully

Arrange the items in an attractive basket or container, placing the homemade gifts front and center.

4. Add Finishing Touches

Decorate the basket with festive ribbon, greenery, or ornaments to enhance its holiday appeal.

Creating personalized gift baskets allows you to tailor your gifts to your recipients' tastes and preferences, making them feel extra special.

With these ideas for thoughtful homemade gifts, packaging and presentation tips, and DIY food gift recipes, you can spread holiday joy and appreciation to your loved ones in a delicious and heartfelt way.

Chapter 16: A German Christmas Eve Dinner Menu

Planning the Perfect Christmas Eve Dinner

Christmas Eve is a time for gathering with loved ones around a festive table, sharing a special meal, and creating cherished memories. In this chapter, we'll guide you in planning the perfect Christmas Eve dinner, provide a selection of recipes to combine for a memorable menu, and share tips for setting the table for a festive feast.

Planning the Perfect Christmas Eve Dinner

Planning a Christmas Eve dinner involves careful consideration of traditions, flavors, and the preferences of your guests. Here are some steps to help you plan the perfect meal:

1. Choose Your Theme

Decide on a theme for your Christmas Eve dinner, such as a traditional German feast or a modern and creative menu.

2. Guest List and Invitations

Determine who will be joining you for the celebration and send out invitations well in advance.

3. Menu Selection

Select a menu that suits your theme and the preferences of your guests. Consider dietary restrictions and allergies.

4. Grocery Shopping

Create a shopping list based on your selected recipes and gather all the necessary ingredients.

5. Preparation Schedule

Plan your cooking schedule to ensure that everything is ready to serve at the desired time.

6. Decor and Table Setting

Choose a festive tablecloth, centerpieces, candles, and dinnerware to set the mood.

7. Entertainment and Activities

Plan activities or entertainment to keep your guests engaged and in the holiday spirit.

Combining Recipes for a Memorable Menu

Creating a memorable Christmas Eve dinner menu is a delightful culinary adventure. Here's a selection of recipes to inspire your menu:

Appetizer:

German Potato Pancakes (Kartoffelpuffer): Crispy potato pancakes served with applesauce and sour cream for dipping.

Soup:

Creamy Chestnut Soup: A velvety soup made with roasted chestnuts, onions, and a touch of cream, garnished with fresh herbs.

Main Course:

Roast Duck with Red Cabbage and Potato Dumplings: Succulent roast duck served with sweet and tangy red cabbage and traditional potato dumplings (Kartoffelklöße).

Side Dish:

Green Bean Almondine: Tender green beans sautéed with butter and toasted almonds, seasoned with lemon zest.

Salad:

Winter Salad with Cranberry Vinaigrette: A refreshing salad featuring mixed greens, dried cranberries, candied pecans, and a homemade cranberry vinaigrette.

Dessert:

Stollen: A traditional German Christmas bread filled with dried fruits, nuts, and marzipan, dusted with powdered sugar.

Beverage:

Eggnog: A creamy, spiced eggnog with a hint of rum or bourbon, garnished with nutmeg.

Combine these recipes to create a harmonious and festive Christmas Eve dinner menu that celebrates the flavors of Germany and the holiday season.

Setting the Table for a Festive Feast

A beautifully set table enhances the dining experience and adds to the festive ambiance of your Christmas Eve dinner. Here are some tips for setting the perfect table:

1. Tablecloth and Linens

Choose a tablecloth in a festive color or pattern that complements your dinnerware.

2. Dinnerware and Flatware

Use your best dinnerware, including plates, bowls, and flatware, for an elegant touch.

3. Glassware

Select appropriate glassware for water, wine, and any other beverages you'll be serving.

4. Centerpiece

Create a stunning centerpiece using fresh flowers, candles, or a decorative holiday arrangement.

5. Place Settings

Arrange place settings with dinner plates, napkins, and utensils for each guest.

6. Name Cards or Favors

Consider adding personalized name cards or small holiday favors at each place setting.

7. Candles

Illuminate the table with candles to create a warm and inviting atmosphere.

8. Music and Ambiance

Play soft holiday music in the background to enhance the ambiance.

With careful planning, a well-crafted menu, and a beautifully set table, your Christmas Eve dinner will be a memorable and joyous occasion for you and your guests.

Chapter 17: Christmas Day Brunch and Breakfast

A Joyful Christmas Morning Spread

Christmas Day begins with a sense of wonder and anticipation. In this chapter, we'll explore the joy of Christmas morning by sharing ideas for a delightful Christmas Day brunch and breakfast. You'll find recipes for a traditional German Christmas breakfast, tips for creating a brunch buffet, and festive morning cocktails and beverages to celebrate the holiday.

A Joyful Christmas Morning Spread

The magic of Christmas morning is best experienced with a delightful spread that warms both the heart and the palate. Here are some elements to consider when planning your Christmas Day brunch:

1. Warm and Cozy Atmosphere

Create a cozy ambiance with soft lighting, candles, and holiday decorations.

2. Inviting Scents

Infuse your home with the comforting aromas of freshly brewed coffee, baking pastries, and sizzling bacon.

3. Festive Music

Play your favorite holiday tunes in the background to set the mood.

4. Family Traditions

Incorporate cherished family traditions, like opening presents or reading a Christmas story, into your morning routine.

5. Joyful Gathering

Encourage family and friends to gather around the table or by the fireplace to share the joy of the season.

Recipes for a German Christmas Breakfast

A traditional German Christmas breakfast is a delightful way to start the day. Here are some recipes to consider:

Stollen French Toast

Turn slices of Stollen (German Christmas bread) into decadent French toast, served with powdered sugar and a drizzle of warm honey.

Scrambled Eggs with Smoked Salmon

Fluffy scrambled eggs paired with smoked salmon, fresh dill, and a dollop of crème fraîche.

German Potato Pancakes (Kartoffelpuffer)

Crispy potato pancakes served with applesauce and sour cream.

Homemade Marzipan Croissants

Fill croissants with a sweet marzipan filling and bake until golden brown.

German Nut Bread

A nutty and hearty bread made with almonds, hazelnuts, and spices.

Creating a Brunch Buffet

If you're hosting a larger gathering for Christmas brunch, consider setting up a buffet to accommodate your guests. Here's how to create a brunch buffet:

Food Stations:

Arrange food stations with different types of dishes, such as a pancake station, an omelette station, and a pastry display.

Chafing Dishes:

Keep hot dishes warm using chafing dishes or slow cookers to maintain the ideal serving temperature.

Beverage Station:

Set up a beverage station with coffee, tea, hot chocolate, and a variety of juices.

Decorative Elements:

Decorate the buffet with festive tableware, linens, and decorative accents to create an inviting presentation.

Labeling and Allergen Information:

Provide labels for each dish and include information about potential allergens for the convenience of your guests.

Festive Morning Cocktails and Beverages

Enhance the celebratory mood with festive morning cocktails and beverages:

Mimosas

A classic brunch cocktail made with equal parts champagne and fresh orange juice.

Eggnog Latte

Espresso or strong coffee combined with creamy eggnog and topped with a sprinkle of nutmeg.

Hot Spiced Cider

Warm apple cider infused with spices like cinnamon, cloves, and star anise.

Peppermint White Hot Chocolate

Creamy white hot chocolate flavored with peppermint extract and garnished with crushed candy canes.

Chapter 18: New Year's Eve Celebrations the German Way

Bringing in the New Year with German Traditions

As the year comes to a close, it's time to bid farewell to the old and welcome the new with joy and celebration. In this chapter, we'll explore how to ring in the New Year the German way by bringing in German traditions, offering party planning tips, and sharing delectable appetizer and finger food recipes to make your New Year's Eve celebrations memorable.

Bringing in the New Year with German Traditions

Germans have a rich history of celebrating New Year's Eve, known as "Silvester." Here are some traditions and customs to consider incorporating into your celebration:

1. Fireworks

Fireworks displays are a common way to mark the transition into the new year in Germany. Host a safe and dazzling fireworks show for your guests.

2. Dinner for Good Luck

Germans believe that eating certain foods like sauerkraut, lentils, and pork on New Year's Eve brings good luck for the coming year. Consider including these dishes in your menu.

3. First Footer Tradition

The "first footer" is the first person to enter a home after midnight. Invite a friend or family member to be your first footer, and it's said to bring luck if they bring small gifts like coins, bread, and salt.

4. New Year's Eve Concerts

Many cities in Germany host outdoor concerts and parties on New Year's Eve. Play festive music or hire a live band to keep the party going.

Party Planning Tips

Hosting a New Year's Eve party requires careful planning to ensure a memorable and enjoyable evening. Here are some tips to help you prepare:

1. Invitations

Send out invitations well in advance to ensure your guests can mark their calendars.

2. Decorations

Decorate your home with a festive theme, including balloons, streamers, and confetti.

3. Countdown Clock

Set up a countdown clock or display to build excitement as the new year approaches.

4. Party Favors

Provide party favors such as hats, noisemakers, and sparklers for guests to enjoy.

5. Safety

Ensure that you have a plan for designated drivers or alternative transportation for guests who may have indulged in alcoholic beverages.

Appetizers and Finger Foods for New Year's Eve

Delight your guests with a selection of appetizers and finger foods that are perfect for snacking throughout the evening. Here are some German-inspired options:

Mini Pretzels with Mustard

Serve bite-sized pretzels with a variety of mustards for dipping.

Sausage Platter

Create a platter with a variety of German sausages, such as bratwurst and weisswurst, served with mustard and sauerkraut.

Bavarian Soft Pretzel Bites

These soft pretzel bites are perfect for dipping in cheese sauce or mustard.

Potato Pancakes (Rösti)

Offer crispy potato pancakes topped with sour cream and chives.

Smoked Salmon Canapés

Top small slices of baguette with cream cheese, smoked salmon, and fresh dill.

Cheese and Charcuterie Board

Create a beautiful display with an assortment of cheeses, cured meats, olives, and crusty bread.

Mini Black Forest Ham Sandwiches

Make small sandwiches with black forest ham, Swiss cheese, and pickles on rye bread.

Vegetable Platter with Dip

Offer an array of fresh vegetables with a creamy herb dip.

Chapter 19: Recipes for a Cozy Christmas Morning

Breakfast-in-Bed Favorites

Christmas morning is a time for warmth, togetherness, and cherished moments with loved ones. In this chapter, we'll explore recipes for a cozy Christmas morning, including breakfast-in-bed favorites, warm drinks and cocktails for a chilly morning, recipes for a relaxing start to the day, and the beauty of Christmas morning traditions.

Breakfast-in-Bed Favorites

There's no better way to start Christmas morning than with a special breakfast in bed. Here are some comforting and indulgent breakfast ideas:

Eggnog Pancakes

Fluffy pancakes made with eggnog and served with a drizzle of maple syrup.

Cinnamon French Toast

Thick slices of French toast dipped in a cinnamon-spiced egg mixture and pan-fried until golden brown.

Homemade Waffles

Crisp and tender waffles topped with fresh berries and a dollop of whipped cream.

Smoked Salmon and Cream Cheese Bagels

Bagels spread with cream cheese and topped with smoked salmon, red onion, capers, and fresh dill.

Breakfast Burritos

Scrambled eggs, sautéed vegetables, cheese, and salsa wrapped in warm tortillas.

Quiche Lorraine

A classic quiche filled with bacon, Gruyère cheese, and a creamy custard.

Warm Drinks and Cocktails for a Chilly Morning

Christmas morning often brings a chill to the air. Warm up with these cozy beverages:

Hot Chocolate

Creamy hot chocolate topped with marshmallows or whipped cream.

Spiced Chai Latte

Fragrant and spicy chai tea with steamed milk and a sprinkle of cinnamon.

Irish Coffee

A blend of hot coffee, Irish whiskey, sugar, and a layer of whipped cream.

Mulled Cider

Warm apple cider simmered with spices like cinnamon and cloves.

Mimosa

A refreshing combination of champagne and fresh orange juice.

Gingerbread Latte

Espresso or coffee infused with gingerbread syrup and topped with frothy milk.

Recipes for a Relaxing Start to the Day

Christmas morning is an opportunity to enjoy a leisurely start to the day. Here are some recipes to help you relax and savor the moment:

Yogurt Parfait

Layer yogurt with granola and fresh fruit for a wholesome and customizable breakfast.

Fruit Salad

A refreshing mix of seasonal fruits tossed in a honey-lime dressing.

Oatmeal with Toppings Bar

Prepare a batch of oatmeal and set up a toppings bar with options like brown sugar, nuts, dried fruits, and maple syrup.

Baked Goods

Enjoy freshly baked muffins, scones, or croissants with butter and jam.

Relaxing Tea

Brew a pot of your favorite herbal tea and sip it slowly as you savor the peaceful morning.

Christmas Morning Traditions

Christmas morning is made even more special with cherished traditions. Here are some heartwarming ideas:

Opening Presents by the Tree

Gather around the Christmas tree to exchange and open gifts.

Reading a Christmas Story

Share a beloved Christmas story or read a holiday-themed book aloud.

Christmas Music

Play your favorite Christmas songs or carols in the background to set the mood.

Creating Handmade Ornaments

Spend time crafting and decorating homemade ornaments as a family.

Writing Letters to Santa

Encourage children to write letters to Santa Claus with their holiday wishes.

Christmas Morning Walk

Take a brisk walk to enjoy the serene beauty of a Christmas morning covered in snow.

Christmas morning traditions create lasting memories and add to the magic of the holiday season.

With these recipes for a cozy Christmas morning, warm drinks and cocktails for a chilly morning, ideas for a relaxing start to the day, and the importance of Christmas morning traditions, you can make the most of this special time with your loved ones.

Chapter 20: Leftover Transformations: Delicious Post-Christmas Meals

Reinventing Leftovers into New Delights

After the holiday feasting, it's time to get creative with your leftovers. In this chapter, we'll explore the art of transforming holiday leftovers into delicious post-Christmas meals. You'll find creative recipes for repurposing leftover ingredients, tips for reducing food waste, and guidance on preserving and freezing leftovers for future enjoyment.

Reinventing Leftovers into New Delights

Leftovers from your festive holiday meals can be transformed into delightful new dishes. Here are some ideas for giving your leftovers a delicious makeover:

Turkey and Cranberry Panini

Layer slices of turkey, cranberry sauce, and brie cheese between two slices of crusty bread, then grill until the cheese is melted and the bread is crispy.

Ham and Cheese Quiche

Dice leftover ham and incorporate it into a savory quiche with cheese and vegetables.

Vegetable Frittata

Combine leftover roasted vegetables, herbs, and eggs to create a flavorful frittata.

Mashed Potato Pancakes

Mix mashed potatoes with grated cheese and chives, form into patties, and pan-fry until golden brown.

Stuffing-Stuffed Mushrooms

Hollow out mushrooms, fill them with leftover stuffing, and bake until they're hot and crispy.

Cranberry Oatmeal Bars

Use leftover cranberry sauce as a filling for oatmeal bars or squares.

Creative Recipes for Post-Holiday Meals

When it comes to repurposing leftovers, creativity is key. Here are some more creative recipes to inspire your post-holiday meals:

Leftover Turkey Pot Pie

Combine turkey, vegetables, and gravy in a pie crust for a comforting pot pie.

Christmas Dinner Sandwich

Layer slices of roast beef, ham, and cheese between bread with a drizzle of leftover gravy.

German Shepherd's Pie

Transform mashed potatoes, sauerkraut, and leftover meat into a German-inspired shepherd's pie.

Turkey and Wild Rice Soup

Simmer turkey and wild rice with vegetables in a hearty soup.

Festive Salad with Cranberry Dressing

Create a salad with leftover greens, roasted vegetables, and a homemade cranberry vinaigrette.

Leftover Cheeseboard

Arrange leftover cheeses, dried fruits, and nuts on a cheeseboard for a casual meal.

Tips for Reducing Food Waste

Reducing food waste is not only environmentally responsible but also a way to maximize your holiday feast. Here are some tips for minimizing food waste:

1. Plan Portions Carefully

Estimate the amount of food needed to avoid excessive leftovers.

2. Share with Guests

Encourage guests to take home leftovers in reusable containers.

3. Label and Date Leftovers

Properly label and date leftovers to keep track of freshness.

4. Use Leftover Ingredients

Incorporate leftovers into your meals or donate excess food to those in need.

Preserving and Freezing Leftovers

To make the most of your holiday leftovers, consider freezing certain items for later use. Here's how to preserve and freeze leftovers effectively:

Packaging

Use airtight containers or freezer-safe bags to store leftovers.

Labeling

Label containers with the contents and date of preparation.

Safety

Freeze leftovers within 2 hours of cooking to maintain food safety.

Reheating

Reheat frozen leftovers in the oven or microwave, following safe reheating guidelines

.

By following these preservation and freezing tips, you can extend the life of your holiday leftovers and enjoy them well into the new year.

With these ideas for reinventing leftovers into new delights, creative recipes for post-holiday meals, tips for reducing food waste, and guidance on preserving and freezing leftovers, you can make the most of the holiday bounty and savor the festive flavors beyond the celebration.

As we come to the end of this culinary journey through a German Christmas, we hope this cookbook has filled your heart and kitchen with the warmth, flavors, and traditions of this cherished holiday season. From the joyful anticipation of Advent to the festive feasts of Christmas Eve and Christmas Day, and even the delightful transformations of post-holiday leftovers, the German Christmas experience is a tapestry of culinary delights and heartwarming traditions.

We've explored the art of crafting delectable holiday desserts, sipped on hot drinks by the fireside, ventured into Christmas markets, and delved into the magic of creating handmade decorations. Through each chapter, we've aimed to capture the essence of a German Christmas, from its rich history to its modern celebrations.

Remember, the heart of any holiday celebration lies in the shared moments with loved ones, the laughter, the stories, and the warmth of togetherness. Whether you've embarked on this culinary adventure to create a traditional German feast or simply to infuse your own celebrations with a touch of German flair, we hope this cookbook has served as a delightful guide.

As you embrace the holiday season with open arms and gather around the table with family and friends, may these recipes and traditions fill your home with love, joy, and the comforting aroma of holiday dishes prepared with care.

Frohe Weihnachten! (Merry Christmas!)

May your holidays be filled with love, laughter, and the delicious flavors of a German Christmas.